E
Hel

Helweg, Hans
Farm animals

DATE DUE

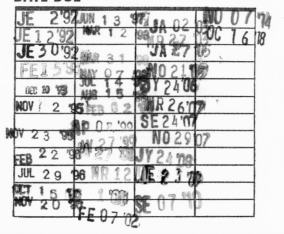

JE 2'92	JUN 13 97	JA 02 0	NO 07 '14
JE 12'92	MR 1 2 98	MR 27 0	OC 16 '18
JE 30'92	MR 31 99	JA 27 06	
FE 15'9	MY 07 99	NO 21 0	
DEC 10 '93	JUL 14 99	JY 24'06	
NOV 2 '95	JUL 15 99 FEB 02	MR 26'07	
NOV 23 '95	AP 05 '00 JN 27 '00	SE 24'07	
FEB 22 '96	N 27 '0	NO 29'07	
JUL 29 '96	MR 12	JY 24'08	
OCT 1 5 '9 1 '00		JE 2 3 '0	
NOV 20 '9 FE 07 '02		SE 07 '10	

Farm Animals

A Random House PICTUREBACK®

Hans Helweg

Farm

Animals

RANDOM HOUSE 🏠 NEW YORK

Copyright © 1978 by Hans Helweg. All rights reserved under International and Pan-American Copyright Conventions.
Published in the United States by Random House, Inc., New York, and simultaneously in Canada by Random House of Canada Limited, Toronto.
Library of Congress Cataloging in Publication Data: Helweg, Hans. Farm animals. SUMMARY: Identifies and explains the usefulness of animals
commonly found on farms. 1. Domestic animals—Juvenile literature. [1. Domestic animals] I. Title. SF75.5.H44 1980 636 79-27483.
ISBN: 0-394-83618-9 (B.C.); 0-394-83733-9 (trade); 0-394-93733-3 (lib. bdg.)
Manufactured in the United States of America A B C D E F G H I J   1 2 3 4 5 6 7 8 9 0

Early in the morning the roosters crow. Then the farmer knows it is time to get up. Roosters strut around the barnyard, acting as if they are in charge of everything. They puff out their chests and look very proud of themselves.

Cows graze in the pasture, eating grass
and clover. Some kinds of cattle are raised
for the milk they give. Other kinds are beef
cattle. They are raised for meat. Male
cattle are called bulls or steers.

In the barn, a mother cow watches over her newborn calf. A calf can drink its mother's milk for nearly a year. But when it is a few days old, the farmer usually starts feeding the calf a special formula. Then people can use the cow's milk.

Goats give good milk, too. It is especially good
for making cheese. The female goat is sometimes
called a nanny goat. The male is called a billy
goat. Baby goats are called kids.

A chicken's eggs take three weeks to hatch.
The mother hen keeps her eggs and her chicks
warm by sitting on them. When a hen finds
something good to eat, she calls her chicks
by making a clucking sound.

Turkeys are bigger than chickens. The male turkey, called a tom, has very fancy feathers. A tuft of feathers hangs from his breast. Most turkeys are sold at holiday time for Thanksgiving and Christmas dinners.

Farmers raise horses for riding or racing. Some horses do heavy farm work, like pulling wagons. A young horse is called a colt. It is fully grown when it is about five years old.

Donkeys and mules are smaller than horses, but they are strong. And they don't eat as much food as horses do. They pull carts and carry heavy loads. Donkeys and mules can sometimes be stubborn, and they also like to kick.

To protect her newborn kittens, a mother cat keeps them in a secret place—sometimes in the hayloft. When the kittens are old enough, she teaches them how to hunt for mice.

Rabbits make good pets, but farmers also raise them for their fur and for meat. Rabbits live in a big, warm hutch on a bed of clean hay. Little rabbit kits like to dig holes into the hay.

Farm geese make a loud honking noise. They are not always friendly.
Underneath their smooth, shiny feathers geese have soft, fluffy
feathers called down. Goose down is used to stuff pillows and quilts.

Full-grown pigs are called hogs. They live in a special pen called a sty. Hogs have small eyes and cannot see very well. But they can smell food from far away!

Ducks have webbed feet that help them swim. Little ducklings stay close to their mother. They can swim and walk on the day they hatch from their eggs.

Sheep stay together in flocks. Their soft fleece is made
into yarn and warm woolen cloth. Male sheep, called rams,
sometimes have big, curved horns. The little lambs
do not have horns yet, but they like to play or
pretend to fight, just like grown-up rams.

A dog can help the farmer herd sheep. The Border collie makes the sheep move to a new pasture or into a pen. At night, when the farm is quiet, the collie guards the sleeping sheep.